Journey Through the Church Year

The Time
of
Christmas

Written by Suzanne Richterkessing • Illustrated by Susan Morris

QualityLife Resources
AAL®

CPH™

Concordia Publishing House
3558 South Jefferson Ave.
Saint Louis, Missouri 63118

© 1999 Aid Association for Lutherans

Published by Concordia Publishing House
3558 S. Jefferson Avenue, St. Louis, MO 63118-3968
Manufactured in the United States of America

2   3   4   5   6   7   8   9   10   08   07   06   05   04   03   02   01   00   99

The cold fall wind sent the leaves skittering across the sidewalk. From under the bush a tiny mouse voice said, "Ohhh, Smudge, I can't stop shivering. Thanksgiving was only a few days ago, but I'm so hungry that my tummy is rumbling."

"I know, Smidge. Even though the farmer dug up our old home, soon we'll find a new home where we'll be safe and warm and happy," Smudge chattered. His stomach growled, too. Then, the two mice spotted a large building with big doors.

The building in front of the two mice looked warm and inviting, but there was just one problem. Smidge and Smudge could not find a way to get inside.

As they stared at the entrance, wondering what to do next, the big doors opened. People of all sizes and ages came out, talking and laughing with one another. Smidge and Smudge noticed nobody was watching so they inched closer and closer to the doors. As the doors were about to close, the mice scampered inside!

"We did it! We did it! We have a home at last!" Smidge and Smudge squealed. They began to celebrate, dancing in circles and chasing each other back and forth across the floor.

"Hold it!" said a loud voice.

The two little mice screeched to a stop. They looked around but didn't see anyone. "Who are you?" they asked. "Where are you?"

"You are curious mice, indeed!" the voice said playfully. "But before you learn about me, I want you to learn more about this wonderful place.

"This is, indeed, a very special house. If you want to live here, there are a few things you will need to know. We'll begin your lessons this instant. Indeed, indeed!"

"Follow me," the voice called. Smidge and Smudge followed the sound into the biggest room they had ever seen.

"Where are we?" asked Smidge.

"You are in God's house," the voice explained. "It is called a church. God's people gather here to worship and praise Him.

"It might be the season of fall outside, but here in God's house the season of Advent is beginning," the voice continued.

"We know fall," said Smidge, "but what is Advent?"

"Ah, I see it is time for your first lesson," said the voice. "Let's move closer to the front and I will begin. Indeed, indeed!"

Advent Season

"Advent is the time when God's people get ready to celebrate Jesus' birth," the voice said. "Advent is also all about promises. Long ago, God promised He would send His Son, Jesus, to be the Savior. God's people hear these words of promise when they listen to the Bible readings."

Suddenly, Smudge spotted a bush hanging in the air. "That's the funniest bush I've ever seen," he said as he laughed. "What is it doing up there?"

"That's not a bush, it's an Advent wreath," the voice explained. "It is hanging up there so everyone can see it. The wreath is a circle with no beginning and no end. It reminds God's people that His love never stops.

"Do you see the four candles?" The two mice nodded. "There is one candle for each of the four Sundays in Advent. A new candle is lit every Sunday. When they are all burning brightly, Jesus' birthday will be very near. Indeed, indeed!"

Smidge and Smudge learned many things about their new home from the voice. They also learned things as they listened to the people who came to church every Sunday. They heard about the angels' messages to Zechariah, Mary and Joseph, and hummed along with the people as they sang.

Early one morning, just about the time the fourth candle on the Advent wreath was lit, Smidge and Smudge awoke to find the church buzzing with activity. People were everywhere, decorating the church with garland and unwrapping ornaments to put on the Christmas tree. Other people were busy working together to set up the nativity scene.

"What's happening?" Smidge wondered aloud.

"I think we should stay here just to be safe," said Smudge. So the little mice watched the activities all day long from a safe corner of the balcony.

Christmas Season

Only when the last person was gone did Smidge and Smudge sneak out of their hiding place and slowly move to the front of the church.

"Look what I found!" Smidge exclaimed. She and Smudge scurried to investigate a small shed with lifelike figures standing inside.

"I think this would be a perfect place for our nest, don't you?" Smidge asked. Smudge nodded his head in agreement.

Before they could start moving in, they heard, "No! Indeed!" The voice startled the little mice.

"This is the nativity scene," the voice said. "It looks like the place where Jesus was born. The figures show Mary and Joseph, Baby Jesus, shepherds and the animals who shared their home with Jesus. It is time to sing and rejoice because Jesus is born. Indeed, indeed!"

The voice told Smidge and Smudge to go to the Christmas tree. It was decorated with white and gold ornaments called chrismons. The voice explained that each chrismon was a symbol for Jesus.

"The crown shows that Jesus is King. The fish stands for Jesus Christ, God's Son, and the lamb reminds God's people that Jesus is the Lamb of God who came to take away the sins of the world," the voice said.

The little mice saw other chrismons too, like stars and many kinds of crosses.

"Why are there so many candles around the church?" Smudge asked.

"The candles are a reminder that Jesus is the Light of the world," the voice told him. "Indeed, indeed!"

Smidge noticed the color on the altar had been changed to white. "White is the color of light and joy," the voice told her. "Christmas is, indeed, the season for hearing God's wonderful message that Jesus, the Savior of the world, was born in Bethlehem. It is time to celebrate His birth." And with that the voice was gone.

During the 12 days of Christmas, the two little mice heard the story of Jesus' birth read from the book of Luke in God's Word, the Bible. They listened with delight to the joyful celebration music. Smidge had to grab Smudge to keep him from toppling off the balcony when he sang, "Angels We Have Heard on High."

They agreed that Christmas was a joyful season. "Indeed, indeed!" said Smidge, giggling.

Smidge and Smudge decided it was time to search for a permanent place for their nest. They agreed one of the empty boxes would be perfect.

Both mice made many trips in and out of the box with bits of ribbon, yarn and cotton balls from the Sunday school rooms, and straw from the nativity scene. Smidge added a tiny foil star as the final touch.

Smidge and Smudge both stood back to admire their new home before crawling inside.

Without warning, the box began to shake and then to move. The mice escaped just in time. Someone picked up their new home along with other empty boxes and carried them away.

"Oh, no!" shrieked Smidge.

"What's going on?" asked Smudge.

"You didn't think Christmas would last forever, did you?" asked the voice. The two young mice jumped and giggled. They were getting used to the voice speaking when they least expected it.

"We like Christmas," the two mice said together.

"Ah, yes, indeed," the voice replied. "Just as winter follows fall, another new season follows Christmas.

"The next season is Epiphany," the voice continued. "See, the people are packing away most of the Christmas decorations. It is such a busy time. Indeed, indeed!"

With that, he was gone.

When all was quiet, Smidge and Smudge crept into the church. Although most of the Christmas decorations were gone, Smudge discovered that some of the nativity scene remained. The shepherds had been replaced by men in royal clothing who were carrying gifts for Jesus. The voice explained that these men were the Magi, or Wise Men, who came from faraway to celebrate Jesus' birth.

Smidge listened as the pastor talked to the children on Sunday. The pastor said, "Epiphany reminds us that Jesus is the Light of the world." He pointed to the star on the Epiphany banner.

On the next Sunday, the pastor told the children about Baptism. He showed them the baptismal font and described how Jesus was baptized in the Jordan River. The pastor pointed to the dove carved into the font. He told how the Holy Spirit appeared in the form of a dove as God said, "This is My Son, whom I love; with Him I am well pleased."

During the weeks of Epiphany, Smidge and Smudge learned many things about Jesus. When they saw something they did not understand, the voice patiently explained it to them.

It was also during Epiphany that Smidge and Smudge found their new home. One quiet evening, they decided to investigate the large wooden box that made the joyful sounds they had heard during Christmas and Epiphany.

Above the box the mice saw a wonderful set of pipes. Climbing into a small pipe, Smidge announced, "This is the perfect place for our nest. Look! It even has a window. From here we can watch everything that goes on in church."

Since Smudge needed no convincing, they began work immediately. The nest was finished in no time at all.

"A church is a wonderful home," said Smidge with a sigh as she nestled down for a well-deserved nap.

Smidge and Smudge had been so busy that they did not notice an older mouse watching them from the organ bench. He had a knowing smile on his face. "Ah, yes. They still have much to learn," he whispered to himself. "Indeed, indeed!"